Fairy things to make and do

Rebecca Gilpin

Designed by Katrina Fearn

Illustrated by Jan McCafferty, Lucy Parris and Molly Sage

Photographs by Howard Allman

Contents

There are lots of shiny silver stickers in the middle of this book.
You can use them to decorate the things you make.

Funky fairies

1. Cut a round head from thin white cardboard. Then, cut a triangle from bright cardboard, for the fairy's body.

2. Cut two bright paper triangles for hair. Then, cut curves along the bottom edges and round off the points at the top.

3. Glue the head onto the body, and glue the hair onto the head, so that the pieces touch at the top. Then, draw a face.

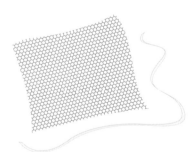

4. Cut a square of pink net for the fairy's wings. Then, cut a long piece of bright ribbon to hang the fairy from.

5. Scrunch the middle of the netting and tie it with one end of the ribbon. Then, cut two long pieces of ribbon, for legs.

6. Turn the body over, and tape the wings onto it, with the long piece of ribbon pointing up. Then, tape the legs on, too.

You could
make lots of
different fairies.

7. To make the arms, bend the bumpy part of a drinking straw and cut it so that both ends are the same length, like this.

8. Press the bumpy part of the straw onto a piece of poster tack. Then, press it onto the back of the fairy, just above the wings.

9. For feet, thread beads onto the fairy's legs and tie knots below them. Then, press a sticker on her head and hang her up.

Fairyland painting

Toadstools

1. Lay some paper towels onto some newspaper. Spread red or pink paint on the paper towels with the back of an old spoon.

2. Cut a potato in half, then carefully cut away the two sides, like this, to make a handle. Press the potato into the paint.

3. Press the potato onto a piece of paper. Then, dip a finger in white paint and print some spots. Using a brush, paint a white stalk.

Daisies and dandelions

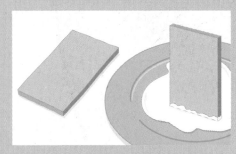  

1. Cut two small pieces of thick cardboard. To print daisies, dip the edge of one piece in white paint and press it on the paper.

2. Print lots more lines and cross them over each other, to make petals. Then, paint a yellow dot in the middle of each daisy.

3. Dip the long edge of the other piece of cardboard in yellow paint and print dandelions. Then, paint stalks and leaves.

Dragonflies

1. To paint a body, dip a fingertip into some paint and drag your finger quickly across the paper. Then, fingerpaint a head.

2. Clean your finger, then dip it in some white paint and drag it to make four wings. Then, add eyes with a felt-tip pen.

Add some fingerpainted fairies to your picture. Print their arms and legs with a piece of cardboard.

Print some toadstools first, then add flowers in the spaces.

Fairy wands

Sparkly star wand

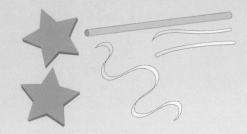

1. Draw a star on a piece of cardboard. Cut it out, then lay it on another piece of cardboard and draw around it twice.

2. Cut out the stars and paint them on one side. Then, cut 10 pieces of thin ribbon which are half as long as a drinking straw.

3. Lay one of the stars on some scrap paper. Then, cover the side which has not been painted with household glue (PVA).

The paper protects the book.

4. Carefully lay the straw and pieces of ribbon on top of the glue, like this. Then, gently glue the other star on top.

5. Lay a sheet of paper over the star. Then, put a heavy book on top, and leave the wand for an hour for the glue to dry.

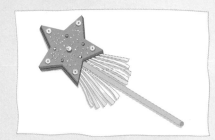

6. Glue lots of sequins, glitter and tiny beads onto one side of the wand. Wait for it to dry, then decorate the other side.

Silver star wand

Make patterns with the string.

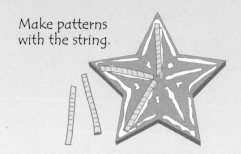

1. Cut out two stars and cover one side of each one with household glue (PVA). Then, press pieces of string onto the glue.

2. Lay a piece of kitchen foil over each star and gently rub all over it. The pattern of the pieces of string appears.

3. When the glue is dry, cut around the stars, leaving a border. Then, cut off the foil at the points, like this.

4. Cut little triangles into the border, like this. Then, bend the border up onto the star, until the edges of the star are covered.

5. Glue pieces of ribbon and a straw onto the back of one star. Then, glue the other star on the top and leave it to dry.

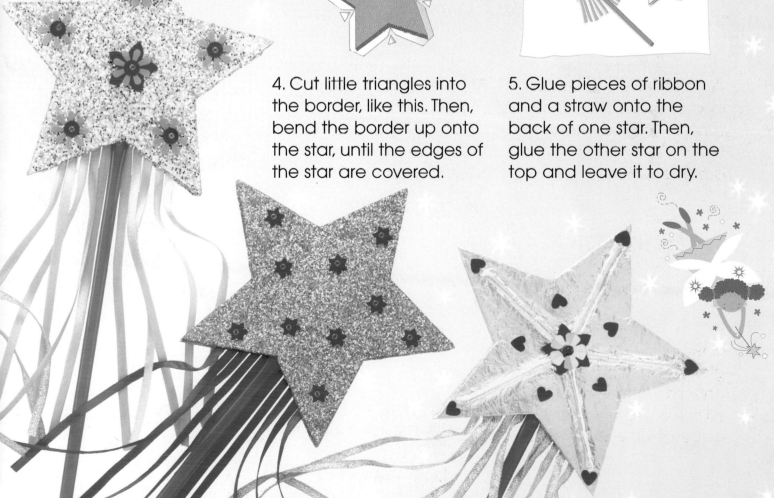

Fairy door sign

Keep this quarter for later.

Remove these parts.

1. Put a small plate onto a sheet of paper and draw around it with a pencil. Then, cut out the circle you have drawn.

2. Fold the circle in half, then in half again, and open it out. Then, cut along two of the folds and remove one quarter.

3. Draw two wings touching the folds. Then, cut around the wings and along the folds to make the wings, like this.

The body stands out from the paper.

4. Decorate the body and the wings. Push the wings together, so the body curves, then glue them onto some thick paper.

Kate's   Room

5. Cut out a head and draw a face. Then, cut out hair and glue it on. Draw two arms on the paper quarter you kept earlier.

Asha's Room

You could glue your fairy onto a heart. Leave room to write your name.

Decorate the sign with shiny stickers.

Decorate the arms.

6. Cut out the arms. Then, cut hands and glue them onto the arms. Glue the arms and the head onto the body.

7. For legs, cut two long strips of paper. Make one end of each leg rounded, then fold the legs lots of times, to make zigzags.

8. Glue the legs under the body, with the rounded ends at the bottom. Then, write your name above the fairy.

Printed fairies

To make a butterfly, cut wings from paper and fold them.

1. Glue a sponge cloth onto a piece of thin cardboard. This helps to make it less messy when you print.

2. Draw a triangle for the body on the cardboard. Then, put a small bottle top on the cardboard and draw around it.

3. Cut around the shapes, through the cardboard and the sponge. Then, lay some paper towels onto some newspaper.

4. Spread white paint on the paper towels, using the back of an old spoon. Then, lay the sponge side of the triangle in the paint.

5. Press the sponge onto a sheet of paper, rub the back gently, then lift it off. Then, print a head and print more fairies.

6. From thin paper, cut enough wing shapes for each fairy to have two. Then, fold each wing in half and open it out.

7. Mix yellow and white paint together to make pale yellow. Then, press the edge of a piece of thick cardboard into the paint.

Leave room for the wings.

The wings stand out a little.

8. Press the cardboard onto the paper to print hair. Then, use another piece of cardboard to print arms and legs.

9. Paint hands and feet, and add faces. Then, spread glue on one half of each wing, and press them on.

To give a fairy curved legs or arms, bend the cardboard before you print.

Flowery fairy wall-hanging

1. Lay a plate on a piece of thick white cardboard. Then, draw around the plate with a pencil and cut out the circle.

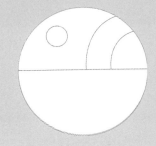

2. Using the pencil, lightly draw a line across the circle. Then, draw the outline of a rainbow and a sun at the top.

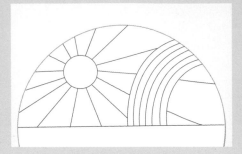

3. Add stripes to the rainbow and lots of lines for the sun's rays, like this. Then, paint bright stripes on the rainbow.

4. Paint the sun and its rays with two shades of yellow paint. Then, paint the ground and leave the paint to dry.

5. Draw lots of flowers on white paper, cut them out and paint yellow circles on them. Then, glue some of them onto the ground.

6. Using the point of a ballpoint pen, carefully make a small hole near the top of the painted circle, like this.

Don't glue flowers at the top of each ribbon.

7. Cut nine long pieces of thin bright ribbon and glue lots of paper flowers onto them. Then, leave the glue to dry.

8. Tape the pieces of ribbon around the bottom of the circle, making sure that you leave gaps between them.

9. Thread a piece of ribbon through the hole in the top of the circle, and tie it in a knot. Then, hang up your wall-hanging.

If you don't want to make a hole in your picture, tape a piece of ribbon to the back instead.

You could draw around the outlines with a silver pen or glitter glue.

You can also hang funky fairies on your wall-hanging (see pages 2-3).

Fairyland butterflies

Salt-speckled butterflies

1. Paint all over a sheet of thick white paper with watery paint. Then, sprinkle grains of salt onto the paint and let it dry.

2. When the paint is dry, brush off the salt. Fold the paper in half and glue it together with the paint on the outside.

The fold needs to be on this side.

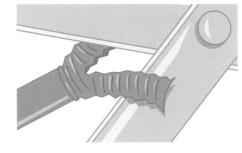

3. Fold the paper in half again. Draw two butterfly wings on it, then cut around the wings, through all the layers of paper.

4. For each butterfly, cut the end off a drinking straw, just above the bumpy part. To make feelers, cut down into the bumpy part.

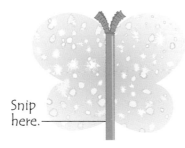

Snip here.

Make sure the bead is wider than the straw.

5. Bend the feelers outward, then open the wings. Lay the straw in the fold, then snip off the bottom end of the straw.

6. Push a piece of ribbon through a bead. Tie a knot in the ribbon and push it through the straw. Glue the straw onto the wings.

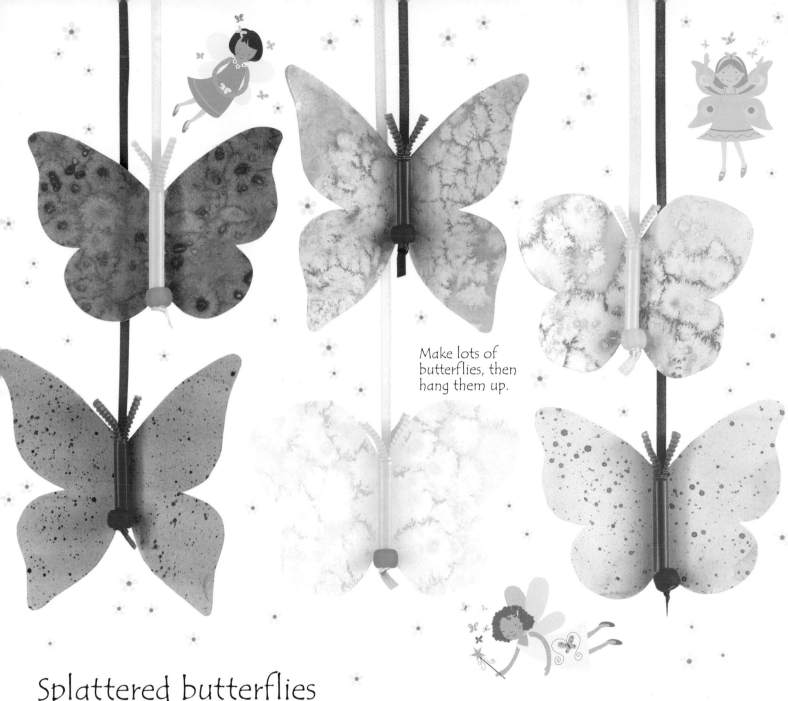

Make lots of
butterflies, then
hang them up.

Splattered butterflies

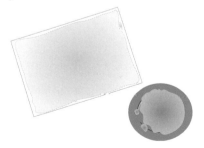

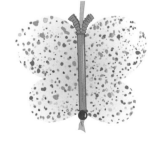

1. Paint all over a sheet of thick white paper with watery paint and let it dry. Then, put some bright paint on an old plate.

2. Dip a dry paintbrush into the paint, then hold it over the paper. Pull a finger over the bristles, to splatter the paint.

3. Splatter paint all over the paper and let it dry. Then, make two butterflies, following the steps on the opposite page.

Fairy pop-up card

Don't press hard.

1. Using a pencil, draw a faint line halfway down a piece of thick paper. Then, draw two wings so that they go over the line.

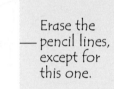

Erase the pencil lines, except for this one.

2. Pressing lightly, draw a body and a head. Add hair, arms and legs. Then, outline the fairy with a felt-tip pen, like this.

Glue on sequins and tiny beads, too, if you like.

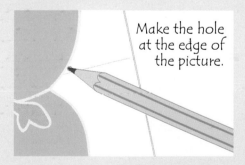

Make the hole at the edge of the picture.

3. Fill in the fairy with pens. Then, carefully press the point of a sharp pencil through the paper, above the pencil line.

Don't cut along the pencil line.

4. Push one scissor blade through the hole. Then, cut carefully around the part of the fairy that is above the pencil line.

The fairy sticks up at the top.

5. To make the card stand up, fold the top part back along the pencil line. Then, decorate the card with pens and stickers.

16

Flower garlands

1. Lay a saucer on some pale pink paper and draw around it. Then, draw around a mug on some bright pink paper.

2. On some white paper, draw around a bottle top. Then, cut out all the circles and glue them together, like this.

To make lots of petals, make more cuts into the circle.

3. For the petals, cut very thin triangles into the biggest circle. Only cut as far as the edge of the bright pink circle.

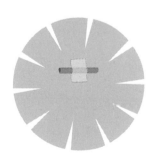

4. Make more flowers, then cut a drinking straw into short pieces. Tape one piece of straw near the top of each flower.

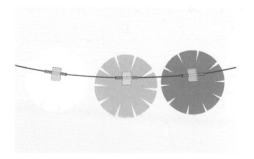

5. With the pieces of straw at the tops of the flowers, thread a long piece of ribbon through them all. Then, hang the flowers up.

Sparkly fairy wings

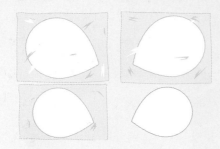

1. Draw two big wing shapes and two smaller ones on paper. Then, cut them out and lay plastic food wrap over them.

2. Rip up two shades of tissue paper and overlap the pieces on the plastic. Cover the wing shapes, including their edges.

3. Mix some household glue (PVA) with water so that it is runny. Then, paint glue all over the pieces of tissue paper.

4. Press on another layer of tissue paper and paint it with glue. Then, add about five more layers of tissue paper and glue.

Put the wings on your back and ask someone to tie the ribbons at the front.

Press on shiny stickers to make the wings even more sparkly.

5. Sprinkle the top layer of glue with glitter. When it is dry, paint another layer of glue over the glitter. Leave the glue to dry.

6. Peel the wings off the food wrap. Lay the paper wings on top, then draw around them and cut out the shapes.

7. Glue the wings together, like this. Then, while the glue is drying, cut a rectangle from some thick cardboard.

8. Using a ballpoint pen, carefully make four holes in the rectangle. Then, thread two long pieces of ribbon through the holes.

Leave long ends on the ribbons.

9. Glue the rectangle onto the back of the wings, with the ends of the ribbons sticking out. Then, let the glue dry.

Flying fairies scene

To make a picture like this, paint toadstools and a fairy castle, then add fairies and flowers.

1. Mix a little orange and pink paint with water, and paint a face. Then, paint a bright pink shape below it for the body, like this.

2. Paint two paler shapes for the fairy's wings. Then, paint a yellow shape for the hair and a circle for the wand.

3. Leave the paint to dry completely. Then, use a black felt-tip pen to add outlines to the fairy's head, body and wings.

More ideas

Piled-up

Spiky

Wavy

Round nose

Freckly

Surprised

4. Draw a face, then add arms, legs and lines on the fairy's hair. Then, draw a wand with a star on the end, like this.

Try painting different hairstyles. Paint a tall shape for piled-up hair, zigzags for spiky hair and curly lines for wavy hair.

Try different faces, too. A few dots make freckles, a round mouth looks surprised and noses can be round or pointed.

21

Fairy puppets

This side of the wing needs to — be on the fold.

1. Fold a piece of thick paper in half. Draw a wing shape on it, like this. Then, keeping the paper folded, cut out the shape.

2. Open out the wings and flatten them. Then, cut a shape for the fairy's body and arms from bright paper.

3. Cut a paper circle for the head and a shape for the hair. Then, glue the hair onto the head and draw a face.

To make your puppets look different, try giving them different dresses and hair.

4. Cut out hands from paper and glue them onto the back of the fairy's arms. Then, glue the head onto the body.

Use pens and stickers to decorate the fairy.

5. Glue the body onto the wings, then decorate the fairy. Turn the fairy over and tape a straw onto the back of the body.

Fairy queen

Make a wand from thick paper and decorate the fairy queen with lots of stickers.

1. Cut a pair of wings from thick paper and lay them on another piece of paper. Draw bigger wings around them, like this.

2. Cut out the wings and glue the smaller wings onto them. Then, cut a long dress, a head, hair and hands from paper.

Draw a face.

3. Glue all the pieces onto the wings. Then, cut a crown from shiny paper and glue it on. Tape a straw onto the back.

Fairy palace

Add extra
decorations to
the palace with
a gold pen.

You could add
some printed fairies
from pages 10-11.

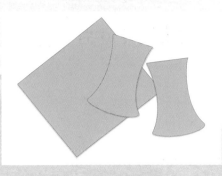

1. Draw a rounded hill on a piece of paper. Draw two more hills, then paint all the hills different shades of green.

2. For the palace, cut a square and two turrets from some paper. Make them small enough to fit on one of the hills.

3. Paint a sun and a sky, then glue the palace onto a hill. Then, cut pink paper roofs and glue them onto the palace.

4. Cut windows and doors from paper and glue them onto the palace. Then, draw frames on them with a felt-tip pen.

5. Cut out small paper hearts and glue one on the top of each roof. Then, paint some trees on the background.

6. Cut out photographs of flowers from magazines and glue them onto the background. Then, draw stalks and leaves.

Fairy tiara

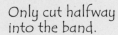
Only cut halfway into the band.

1. Cut a narrow band of thin cardboard that fits once around your head. Then, cut a little off one of the ends.

2. A little way from one end, make a cut going down into the band. Then, make a second cut going up into the other end.

3. Cut six strips of foil which are twice as wide as the band. Then, squeeze and roll them to make thin sticks.

You could use shiny cardboard for the band.

You can bend the foil sticks in lots of different ways to make different kinds of tiaras.

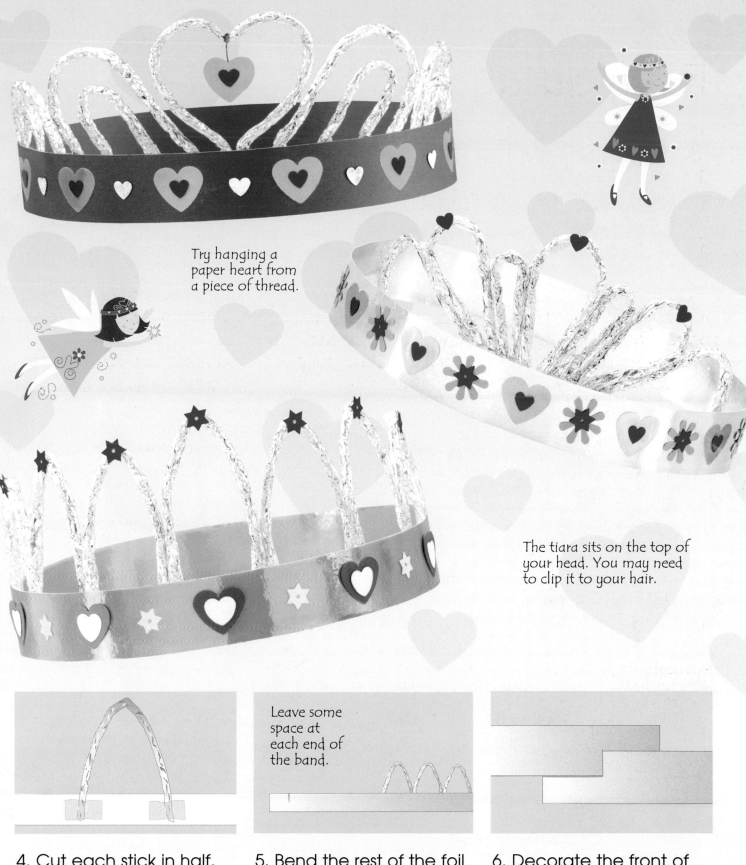

Try hanging a paper heart from a piece of thread.

The tiara sits on the top of your head. You may need to clip it to your hair.

Leave some space at each end of the band.

4. Cut each stick in half. Then, bend one piece in half so that it makes an arch. Tape it onto the middle of the band.

5. Bend the rest of the foil sticks and tape five arches on either side of the middle one. Then, turn the tiara over.

6. Decorate the front of the tiara with stickers and sequins. Then, slot its ends together so that the ends are inside, like this.

Fairy collage

Use paint that isn't too runny.

1. For the wings, lay a small leaf onto some newspaper, with the veins facing up. Then, brush paint over the leaf.

2. Lay the leaf on a piece of tissue paper and press hard all over it with your fingertips. Print six more leaves and let them dry.

You may need to overlap the leaves.

3. Cut out all the printed leaves. Then, cut a pale paper circle for a head. Cut some hair for the fairy from shiny paper.

4. Glue the hair onto the head, and add a face. Then, from bright paper, cut a top and a skirt for the fairy's dress.

5. Glue the skirt onto the top. Then, glue three printed leaves onto the skirt. Cut a strip of paper for a sash, and glue it on.

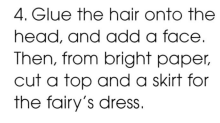

6. From pale paper, cut two arms and glue them to the back of the body. Then, glue on four leaves for the fairy's wings.

7. Turn the body over and glue it onto a piece of paper, but don't glue the bottom of the skirt yet. Then, glue on the head.

8. Cut two shoes from shiny paper and glue them just under the fairy's skirt. Glue the bottom of the skirt onto the paper.

You can use any bright or shiny paper, such as wrapping paper, for the dress.

Make fairies with different hairstyles and crowns.

To make a layered skirt, cut an extra layer and glue it underneath.

9. Cut a crown and a wand from shiny paper and glue them on. Then, decorate the fairy with lots of shiny stickers.

29

Fairyland caterpillar and flowers

Caterpillar

You don't need the lid.

1. Carefully cut the lid off a cardboard egg carton. Then, cut the bottom part of the carton into two pieces, along its length.

2. To make the caterpillar, paint one piece green, and leave it to dry. Put the other piece to one side, for the flowers.

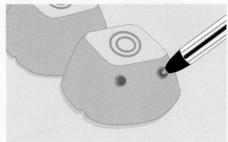

3. Carefully push the point of a ballpoint pen into the front of the caterpillar to make two holes for its feelers.

4. Push two short pieces of drinking straw through the holes. Then, draw a face. Press stickers all over the caterpillar's body.

You could paint spots instead of using stickers.

Make flowers with different petal shapes.

Flowers

1. For the middles of the flowers, cut the other piece of egg carton into three pieces. Paint them orange and let them dry.

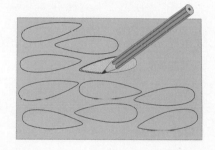

2. Draw a petal on thin cardboard and cut it out. Then, draw around it lots of times on bright paper and cut out the shapes.

3. Turn the orange pieces over and glue the petals onto them, overlapping the petals a little. Then, leave the glue to dry.

4. Scrunch up three pieces of yellow tissue paper. Then, glue them into the middles of the orange sections.

5. For the stalks, press a piece of poster tack onto the back of each flower. Then, press a straw into the poster tack.

More card ideas

You can make lots of different cards
using the techniques in this book.
Here are some ideas you can try:

Bend cardboard
to make frizzy
hair for a printed
fairy (see pages
10-11).

To make
a fairy
collage
card, see
pages
28-29.

Make a mini fairyland
like the one above by
following the steps on
pages 4-5.

Follow the steps on
pages 20-21 to paint
three flying fairies
on a long card.

Make a pretty gift
tag with flowers
from magazines
(see pages 24-25).

Series editor: Fiona Watt • Art director: Mary Cartwright • Photographic manipulation: Emma Julings
Images of flowers on pages 24-25 and page 32 © Digital Vision.
First published in 2003 by Usborne Publishing Ltd., Usborne House, 83-85 Saffron Hill, London, England. www.usborne.com Copyright © 2003 Usborne Publishing Ltd.